Whose Poop Is *THAT?*

Darrin Lunde

Illustrated by **Kelsey Oseid**

◠ Charlesbridge

Whose poop is *that*?

It has bits of bone
and a tuft of fur in it.

A red fox's.

A red fox eats
small mammals and birds.
It crunches their bones
and swallows
their fur or feathers.

Whose poop is *that*?

It is a big pile
with twigs
and stems in it.

An African elephant's.

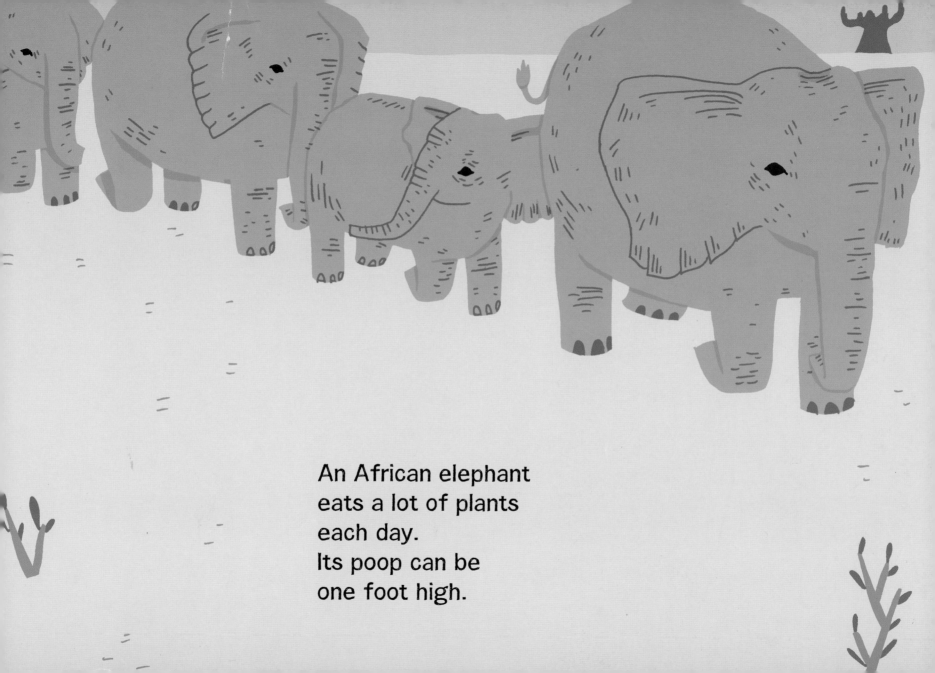

An African elephant
eats a lot of plants
each day.
Its poop can be
one foot high.

Whose poop is *that*?

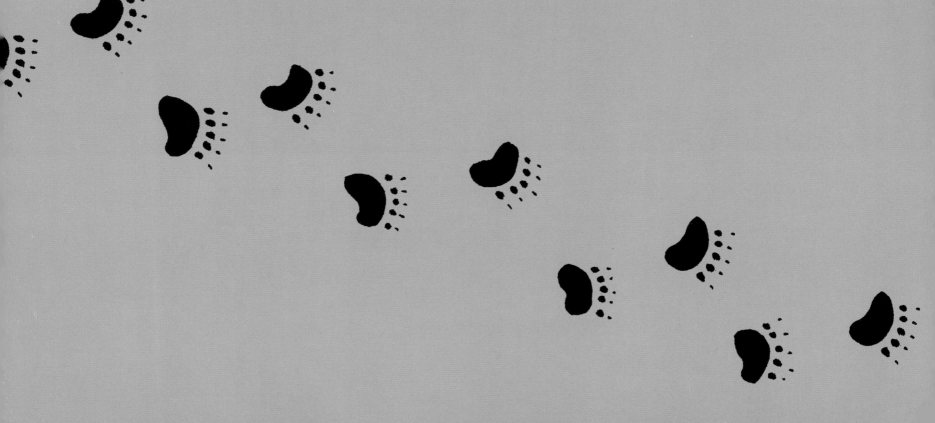

It has a bunch
of splinters in it.

A panda's.

A panda eats
mostly bamboo.
A panda has to spend
most of its day eating
in order to get
enough energy.

Is *that* a poop?

It is a bundle
of fur and bones.

That is *not* a poop.

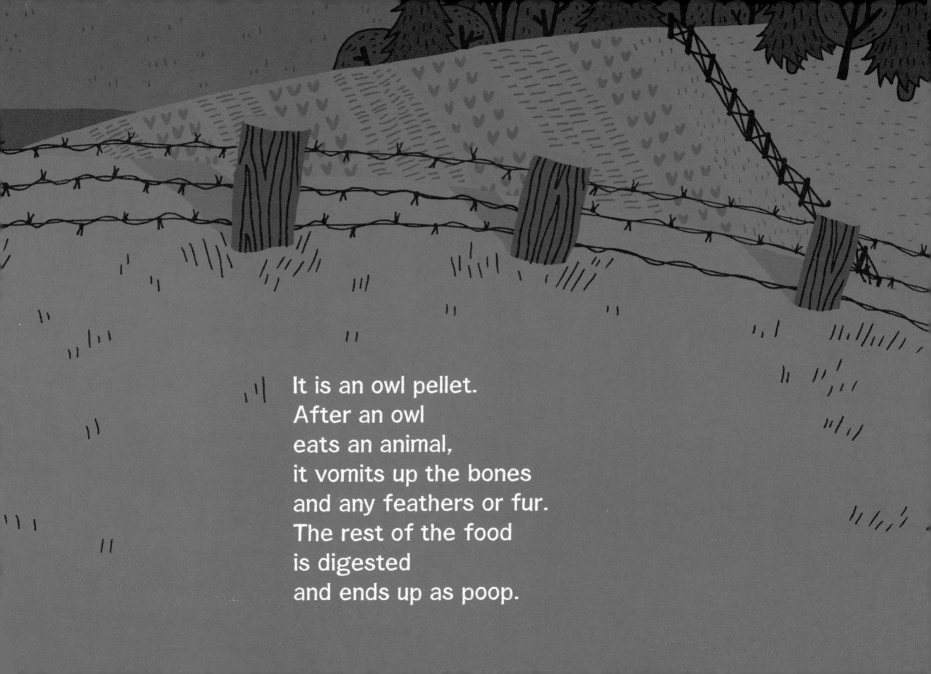

It is an owl pellet.
After an owl
eats an animal,
it vomits up the bones
and any feathers or fur.
The rest of the food
is digested
and ends up as poop.

Whose poop is *that*?

It is full of
old leaves.

A Galápagos tortoise's.

Food needs
at least one week
to pass through
a Galápagos tortoise.
A Galápagos tortoise
sometimes holds its poop
for up to a month.

SPLAT!
Whose poop is *that*?

It dropped
from the sky.

A gull's.

Birds do not need
to land to poop.
Their poop
is very watery.

Whose poop is that?

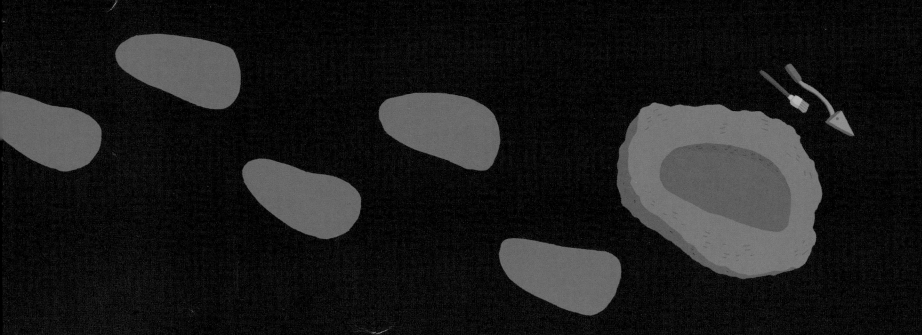

It is as hard
as a rock.

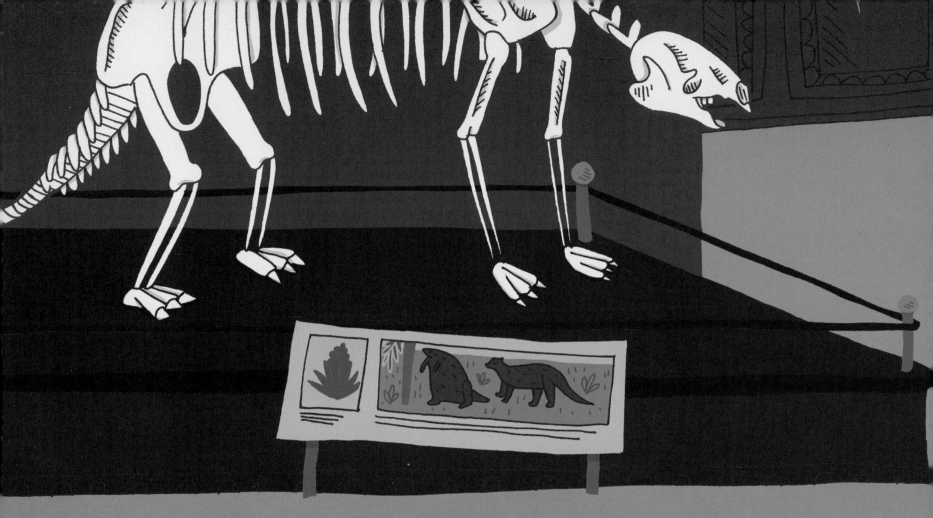

An extinct ground sloth's.

Fossil poop
is hard to find.

You can learn
a lot from poop.
You just have to look!

The Scoop on Poop

- Poop is the waste an animal needs to remove from its body. It includes undigested food and some dead cells from inside the intestines.
- Poop helps return nutrients to the soil. Animal poop can make it easier for plants to grow.
- A plant can spread its seeds when an animal eats its fruit. When the animal poops out the seeds in a different spot, new plants grow.
- Scientists can test poop to find out what an animal was eating and whether it was healthy.
- Poop can spread disease. Worms, bacteria, and viruses can all be spread in poop. You should never touch poop.

Animal Poop Facts

- A rabbit sometimes eats its poop in order to digest its food twice. It gets more energy from its food this way.
- Some people feed coffee beans to an animal called a civet (SIH-vet). When the civet poops out the hard seeds, people grind them to make a special kind of coffee.
- The blue-footed booby bird does not make a typical nest. It lays its eggs on the ground and then makes a ring of its poop around them.
- A fox uses poop to mark its territory. It drops its poop where it will be noticed, such as on top of logs and rocks.
- A fossil poop is called a coprolite (KAH-pruh-lite).

Bonus poop:
Wombat poop is cube shaped!

Oops! Watch your step!

This one is for Buddy. Woof, woof!—D. L.
To Jamie and Fiona. Meow!—K. O.

Text copyright © 2017 by Darrin Lunde
Illustrations copyright © 2017 by Kelsey Oseid
All rights reserved, including the right of reproduction in whole or in part in any form.
Charlesbridge and colophon are registered trademarks of Charlesbridge Publishing, Inc.

Published by Charlesbridge
85 Main Street
Watertown, MA 02472
(617) 926-0329
www.charlesbridge.com

Library of Congress Cataloging-in-Publication Data
Names: Lunde, Darrin P., author. | Oseid, Kelsey, illustrator.
Title: Whose poop is that? / Darrin Lunde; illustrated by Kelsey Oseid.
Description: Watertown, MA: Charlesbridge, [2017] | Description based
   on print version record and CIP data provided by publisher; resource not viewed.
Identifiers: LCCN 2015045099 (print) | LCCN 2015043913 (ebook)
   | ISBN 9781607348801 (ebook) | ISBN 9781607348818 (ebook pdf)
   | ISBN 9781570917981 (reinforced for library use)
Subjects: LCSH: Animal droppings—Juvenile literature. | Animal behavior—Juvenile literature.
Classification: LCC QL768 (print) | LCC QL768 .L86 2017 (ebook) | DDC 591.5—dc23
LC record available at http://lccn.loc.gov/2015045099

Printed in China
(hc) 10 9 8 7 6 5 4 3 2

Illustrations done in pen and ink and colored digitally
Display type set in Graphen by Maciej Wloczewski
Text type set in Franklin Gothic Hand Light by Gert Wiescher, Wiescher-Design
Color separations by Colourscan Print Co Pte Ltd, Singapore
Printed by 1010 Printing International Limited in Huizhou, Guangdong, China
Production supervision by Brian G. Walker
Designed by Martha MacLeod Sikkema